First published in the UK by Sweet Cherry Publishing Limited, 2024
Unit 36, Vulcan House, Vulcan Road,
Leicester, LE5 3EF, United Kingdom

Sweet Cherry Europe (Europe address)
Nauschgasse 4/3/2 POB 1017
Vienna, WI 1220, Austria

2 4 6 8 10 9 7 5 3 1

ISBN: 978-1-80263-153-1

Football Rising Stars: Georgia Stanway

© Sweet Cherry Publishing Limited, 2024

Text by Harry Meredith
Illustrations by Sophie Jones

www.sweetcherrypublishing.com

Printed and bound in Turkey

MIX
Paper from
responsible sources
FSC® C151955

GEORGIA STANWAY

THE UNOFFICIAL STORY

Written by

HARRY MEREDITH

Sweet Cherry

CONTENTS

RECORD GOALSCORER

On the 29th of January 2022, Manchester City travelled to the city of Nottingham. The club were visiting the East Midlands as they had been drawn against Nottingham Forest in the fourth round of the FA Cup. It was one of the most prestigious domestic

cup competitions in the entire country.

Manchester City were expecting to win this match. After all, they were one of the top teams in the country. They regularly competed at the top of the Women's Super League and were in constant pursuit of more trophies. Nottingham Forest, on the other hand, were playing their football in the third tier of the women's game, the FA Women's National League North.

With this in mind, the Manchester

 City manager decided to rotate her team, and give some of the players on the

fringe of the first team an opportunity to play. Georgia Stanway was among the regular players who were named as a substitute for this match. Although Georgia understood the decision and was more than happy to see other players given a chance, she couldn't help but feel disappointed that she might not make it onto the football pitch that day. The talented attacking midfielder was only one strike away from equalling the club's goalscoring record.

Nikita Parris, Georgia's former teammate, currently held the record.

She had scored an incredible sixty-two goals for Manchester City during her stint with the club. Now Georgia was sitting on sixty-one and she only needed one more goal to match Parris's scoresheet. Georgia tried to push her frustration to the back of her mind, but she couldn't quite shake it. She wanted to break that goalscoring record and make it her own.

When a team make multiple changes for a match such as this one, it can leave the door wide open for a cup upset, but Manchester City were up for the game ahead and didn't

take it lightly. They didn't want to sleepwalk into a surprise cup exit. So, as the referee blew the whistle and the match kicked off, Manchester City started the game with unstoppable determination and a clear desire to win. It didn't take them long to make their mark on the match.

In the 2nd minute, Caroline Weir gave the visitors the lead, striking the ball into the net after a cutback from Lauren Hemp. After scoring so early, Manchester City had their opponents firmly on the back foot, and they were determined to keep the pressure up.

The visitors launched attack after attack and were able to build on their lead with two more goals before half-time. Strikes from Khadija Shaw and Filippa Angeldahl put Manchester City into a comfortable 0-3 lead.

At half-time, a delighted Georgia was told she would be playing in the second half. She stretched and ran sprints and got her mind into the game. As both sides emerged from the tunnel to start the second half, Georgia tried to put the thought of getting her name into the Manchester City history books aside and focus

on the match ahead. She
was determined to find an
opportunity in a game already flowing
with goals to find just one more.

Only minutes after Georgia was
introduced into the match,
Manchester City created a chance.
The ball was launched into the penalty
box and Shaw controlled it with her
chest before bringing the ball to her
feet. A defender was at her back,
trying to steal the ball, so Shaw laid
the ball off to Georgia who had made
a darting run into the penalty box.
Georgia took the ball in her stride

and ran to the byline.
She knew the space
was closing on her, so she
looked to her side to try and find
a teammate to cross to. With only
centimetres of the pitch remaining,
Georgia fired in a powerful cross –
but to her surprise, her shot found
the net! Georgia's cross had flown
through the narrowest of gaps,
evading the goalkeeper's glove and
the thwack of the post.

Realising what had happened, a
delighted Georgia ran to the corner
and celebrated, followed quickly

by her teammates. They high-fived and came together to congratulate Georgia on not only scoring but equalling the record. Manchester City were 0-4 up and in complete control of the match. As Georgia jogged back into position to carry on with the remainder of the match another thought crept into her head. There were still forty minutes to go ... would she ... could she ... score another goal and beat the record?

In the 53rd minute, Hemp also added her name to the Manchester City scoresheet, as she fired in a strike

with her formidable left foot. In the 69th minute, a poor touch from the goalkeeper allowed Shaw to fire in her second goal of the match and to make the score 0-6. But it was what happened next that changed everything.

Georgia was the first to meet a fizzed cross into the box and she connected well with the ball, forcing it between the legs of the goalkeeper and straight into the back of the net. The stands echoed with loud roars as the away fans cheered and applauded as they realised what they had just witnessed. The game might have already been won, but this particular goal meant Georgia had smashed the Manchester City goal scoring record. Georgia pumped her fists in the air as she celebrated not only the seventh goal of the match, but even more importantly, the goal that made her Manchester City's all-time top female goalscorer.

In the final minute of the match, Georgia rounded off the perfect day for herself, the team and the fans with one more surprise, as she scored

her third goal with a left-footed strike inside the penalty box. Not only did this add to her tally as the club's top goalscorer, but she had achieved what most attacking players dream about before every match: scoring a hat-trick to help their team emerge victorious. The Manchester City fans went wild as Georgia and her teammates celebrated.

Shortly afterwards, the referee blew the whistle. The game was over, putting the home side out of their misery and giving Manchester City the chance to enjoy their win. It also gave Georgia a moment to take in exactly what she had just achieved.

It was only a handful of years earlier that Georgia had put on a Manchester City shirt for the first time. She had been welcomed with open arms and allowed to flourish under top management and alongside world-class players. Now Georgia had proved not only that she deserved her place in this team, but that she was one of the club's most talented players and an official record breaker. And Georgia was nowhere near finished. Top goalscorer was a title to enjoy and celebrate, a moment to

cherish and be recognised, but it was also a fresh start for the player. It was a taste of what she could achieve in the world of football and Georgia wanted more of it.

If she could become a club's record goalscorer at only the age of twenty-three, who knew what Georgia could achieve during the remainder of her career? It was clear to the whole world that she was not only an exceptional talent, but a player who most would fear having to play against. The first record had been smashed, and now it was time for Georgia to break some more.

2
MIXED MATCHES

Georgia Stanway was born in Barrow-on-Furness on the 3rd of January 1999. She grew up in a port town in the north-west of England as part of a football mad family. With three older brothers and a dad who loved the game, Georgia was always going to get pulled into the excitement and wonder of the footballing world.

One of Georgia's older brothers played for a local team called Furness Rovers. Every weekend, Georgia and her mum would go and watch him play. The three-year-old Georgia watched the matches with fascination and rarely took her eye off the action on the pitch. She would often wait behind the goals and giggle with excitement when a shot went wide or over the crossbar. Georgia loved nothing better than chasing after the loose ball and kicking it back onto the

pitch. At other times, she'd
be found kicking spare balls
along the touchline with the players
on the bench or the watching parents.

As Georgia started to grow, her love
of the game grew with her. Georgia's
mum decided to ask the Furness Rovers
coach if her daughter would be able
to join one of the teams. It wasn't a
usual request as the side was made up
entirely of boys, but the coach could see
how much it meant to Georgia and he
said yes. So, at the age of just four years
old, Georgia was able to move from the
sideline and onto the training pitch.

Georgia was trained at a place known locally as the Strawberry Grounds. When she turned six, she was allowed to play in mixed team matches – games where both boys and girls can play on the same team. Despite Georgia's enthusiasm, training was tough. For a long time, some people believed that only boys should play sports like football. Luckily, such views were starting to fade away, but some still held on to them and refused to accept that girls could do anything that boys could do. Some

of the boys Georgia played against felt the need to prove that they were better than her. They'd dive into tackles and chose not to pass to her whenever any other players were available. But Georgia refused to let this get to her and gave training her all. She shrugged it off and decided to let her football skills do the talking. Session after session, Georgia steadily improved, demonstrating just how much talent and ability she possessed. Every time she walked onto the pitch, she was determined to keep getting better and to develop her game.

Before long, Georgia was one of the best players on the team.

By the time Georgia turned eight, it was clear to the coaches that she was an incredibly special player. They could see that she had something extra that shone whenever she was on her beloved football pitch. Even more impressively, Georgia wasn't just great at one particular thing such as attacking or defending. It was her all-round game that was the most impressive. She excelled in many aspects of football which made her a fearsome opponent.

It was also clear to Georgia's parents that their daughter's talents were starting to outgrow her current situation. She was desperately in need of a new challenge that would allow her to push herself against other talented players in order to take her game up a notch. They started to look for somewhere that Georgia's skills could be developed and nourished. Luckily her skill hadn't gone unnoticed by the wider

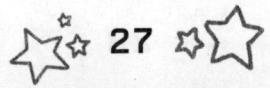 footballing community, and Georgia was invited to join an academy where she

would be able to face off against other top players from the north-west. It was time for Georgia to move from playing in mixed matches to testing herself against some of the best girls in the country.

3

BLACKBURN ROVERS ACADEMY

At thirteen years old, Georgia made the move to the Blackburn Rovers Academy, otherwise known as a regional centre of excellence. It wasn't easy because the academy was over two hours away from Georgia's home. This meant a four-hour round trip, not to mention the actual three-hour training session. But Georgia's parents wanted to do everything they could to help their daughter succeed.

Every week, Georgia attended multiple training sessions with Blackburn. Luckily her school was very understanding and gave the young footballer special permission to leave early in order for her to make the long journey. Georgia would often have to finish her homework in the back of the car as it travelled along the winding and hilly roads. Yet each day she stepped out of the car with a huge smile on her face, determined to work hard and keep on improving her game.

When Georgia first arrived at the centre of excellence, the coaches saw her as a player who had a lot of raw talent. She had obvious ability, but she still needed to be shaped and improved. But they were impressed to see that Georgia needed no help with her desire to be the best or how hard she was prepared to work to

achieve her dreams. They could see
that Georgia never gave anything less
than one hundred percent. With all
these things combined, the coaches
knew that Georgia was something
very special indeed and had a real
chance of making it to the very top of
the footballing world.

Despite being small in size, Georgia
was a fierce and powerful player
and knew exactly how to use her
body on the pitch. She never shied
away from having the ball at her
feet or attempting a shot or pass.
Throughout her time at the centre,

Georgia showed everyone that she was tough, hard-working, athletic and had a huge amount of footballing intelligence. These were exactly the qualities that players needed in order to succeed at a professional club.

Georgia loved her time at the academy. In addition to learning from great coaches, Georgia was able to test herself against some incredibly talented players. Keira Walsh and Ella Toone, two future England internationals, were at the centre of excellence at the same time, which meant she was able to compare her footballing skills against some of the best young girls in the country. This was crucial for Georgia's development as she was constantly challenged and pushed to improve by young women who wanted to become professional footballers as much as she did.

It was clear that some of the group were going to go on to achieve big things, but the centre went out of its way to keep all the girls down-to-earth and level-headed. Georgia and the other players had to pick up the cones, put the nets up and collect the corner flags. This meant

that the whole team were glued together by hard work and a sense of togetherness. They also knew they were lucky enough to be taught by coaches who were dedicated to improving and developing women's football. The coaches wanted nothing more than to help the players go on to play at the highest level, on the world stage.

Under such guidance, Georgia flourished in the academy. She was very much seen as an attacking player but was tested in many positions. But it didn't matter if Georgia played as a number 7, 8, 9, 10 or 11 or whether she was placed across different lines of attack such as a striker, winger or central attacking midfielder, she excelled at them all. No matter where she was on the pitch, Georgia was a player who could make the difference and could help her side find the back of the net and win matches.

Georgia was also one of the feistiest players at the academy. She was incredibly competitive and went out of her way to stand up for herself and her teammates. She was never afraid to bite back. This spirit was something that Georgia needed to learn how to control, as too much could lead to yellow cards or, even worse, red cards resulting in a player being sent off the pitch. She had to be able to channel her passion in a positive way.

As Georgia's time with the academy continued, she was able to hone and improve her talents year after year. Finally, the coaches knew that her time at the academy was over. After three years with the centre of

excellence, the coaches were in no doubt that now was the moment for sixteen-year-old Georgia to progress to the women's game and show what she could do as part of the Blackburn Rovers first team.

4
FIRST TEAM FOOTBALL

Georgia's coaches had been watching her score countless goals for the academy and believed that now was the time for her to make the step up. Georgia was ready to start playing matches for the first team.

Georgia was super excited to

play for Blackburn Rovers, but she couldn't help but feel nervous too. She was going to play in competitive matches that mattered, rather than training games or academy fixtures. Blackburn were in the FA Women's Premier League, the third division of women's football in the country underneath the two divisions of the Women's Super League. This meant that Georgia wouldn't be playing in matches against the country's best footballers, but she was still playing in matches against incredibly experienced and talented women.

But Georgia had no need to worry, as she fitted into first team football quickly and effortlessly. She made five appearances for Blackburn and scored an astonishing six goals in that time. The young star wasn't just performing well, she was thriving within the women's game. The coaches had been right. It was clear that even at such a young age, Georgia was ready to take the step up to women's football. And as she approached her seventeenth birthday, the club were preparing to offer her an official contract and make Georgia a contracted Blackburn Rovers player. But as always in football, things were not going to be quite that simple.

A few days before Georgia's birthday, she was at home with her family getting ready for what seemed like just another ordinary day. But all of that changed when the phone in the kitchen rang. Someone had a question for Georgia that would change everything for ever.

5
THE CALL

Georgia's mum wasn't expecting a phone call and almost didn't answer it. She was sure it was going to be someone trying to sell something that the Stanways could do without. But some sixth sense made her pick up the phone and start an incredible chain of events for Georgia.

The person on the other end of the line turned out to be a representative for Manchester City. They were not only a hugely successful club in the world of football but were heavily investing in improving and developing their women's side. The representative introduced themselves as Manchester City's women's team manager, Nick Cushing. He wanted to set up a meeting with Georgia the following day. He also offered to travel all the way to Georgia's home the following day to see her. This was a sign of just how

much he wanted Georgia on his team, as most meetings took place at the club itself.

True to his word, Cushing arrived at the Stanway home the next afternoon. Georgia had only just returned from school for the day, so she met the manager with a rucksack on her back, her buttons fastened all the way and with a neat tie dangling from her collar. The whole family sat stunned as the manager of one of the country's top football sides did his best to persuade Georgia to join the club.

During the early discussions, and whirlwind first forty-eight hours, Georgia thought that she was being recruited to play for the team's academy, the development squad or at best for their reserves. Never in her wildest dreams did she imagine that they wanted her for the first team. But it soon became clear that Manchester City wanted to bring Georgia in as an attacking option for the main playing squad. She would be able to develop and learn alongside some of the world's very best female football players, while getting to make her mark as one of the country's most exciting young prospects. Georgia could hardly believe it when she finally understood that she was being asked to sign for the team.

Georgia was over the moon. This was a dream come true for any player. However, mixed in with her excitement, she felt a small pinch of fear and apprehension. She would be joining a side filled with talented players but would be leaving everyone and everything she had grown to know and love.

She would have to say goodbye to the many coaches and players she had become close to during her time at the centre of excellence. But despite all this, Georgia didn't hesitate to say yes. She was being offered the chance to play for a team in the top division of women's football in England and to challenge herself in the Women's Super League. There was only ever going to be one outcome. Georgia was going to Manchester City.

6

STARSTRUCK

A few months later, the international players returned to their teams following the 2015 World Cup, and Georgia swapped the countryside for city life. Georgia had been able to travel back and forth to Blackburn, but Manchester was just too far away. Georgia had no choice but to leave

 home and move in with a host family. She was also used to being surrounded by green fields so moving to a city was a big step. It was an incredibly nerve-wracking time for the young player. Georgia's parents packed the car full of all her stuff so she could take it to her new house. Meeting her host family was incredibly daunting but they welcomed her with open arms and made her feel at home straightaway. They made sure she was enrolled in her new school and had everything she needed.

Georgia spent her time studying as hard as she could during the day, before heading to the training ground the moment the bell rang.

Georgia was no longer playing with footballers who she had grown up with, now she was surrounded by famous and recognisable faces. Georgia couldn't believe that she got to train on the same pitch as Lucy Bronze, Karen Bardsley, Demi Stokes, Jennifer Beattie, Jill Scott and England captain Steph Houghton. Georgia was constantly starstruck, although she did her best to hide it.

Only a few months ago some of these players had been Georgia's idols, now they were Georgia's teammates.

Georgia did everything she could to learn from her teammates. If one player made a successful run, a tackle or an innovative move, Georgia would try to do the same. The established players found it endearing. She obviously wanted to do everything she could to learn from everyone around her and to prove that she deserved a place in this squad overflowing with talent.

Georgia and her teammates quickly

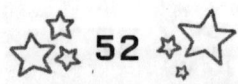

became friends and her
new club started to feel like
home. This was helped by
a handful of team bonding
days that the club put in place. One
day, the team went kayaking. They
were all having the time of their
lives on the river, when suddenly the
heavens opened and it started to pour
with rain. Droplets of water thrashed
down onto the boats and drenched
Georgia and her new teammates.
Rather than run for shelter, the
players laughed and splashed each
other, enjoying the fun and chaos.

Georgia was so wet that she decided to jump into the water. Times like this meant that something special was developing at Manchester City. The players were becoming a tight-knit group of friends who got on incredibly well. And now they had Georgia on their team – a special talent, ready to play a key role in the future of Manchester City.

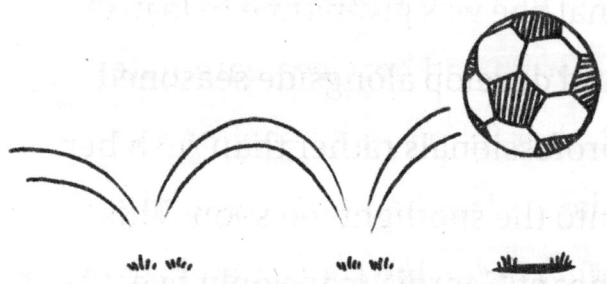

7

THE DOUBLE

It took a while before Georgia was
introduced into the Manchester City
starting lineup. It was important
that she was given time to learn
and develop alongside seasoned
professionals rather than rush her
into the spotlight too soon. This
meant Georgia made only five

appearances for her new team during the club's 2015 campaign, but she still  made her mark. She netted her first competitive goal for the side in a Women's League Cup match away to Everton. And if that wasn't enough, Georgia went on to score her first ever Women's Super League strike in a 6-1 victory against Bristol Academy.

During this season, Manchester City achieved their highest ever league finish in second place. Disappointingly, they were pipped to the league title on the final day,

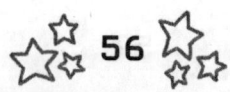

meaning the champions that year were Chelsea. But it was far from a wasted season, as Manchester City had earned themselves qualification into the Champions League for the first time in the club's history. This gave the side plenty of motivation to continue their growth and achieve success.

In the 2016 season, Georgia started to become much more of a recognisable face within the team. She was not a starter for every match, as there were still many experienced players in her position, but she was definitely starting to hold her own.

Every time Georgia was on the pitch, she continued to make her case for a place not just as a substitute, but as a player who could make all the difference for Manchester City.

Over the course of the season Georgia made eleven appearances across all competitions and scored an impressive six goals. Her goal in the 4-1 victory against the Doncaster Belles in the League Cup helped the side progress to the next round. Georgia did not play in the final, but she had played her part in helping the team achieve their first trophy of the season and earned her first ever professional winners' medal. But the season was far from over, nor were the trophies. Manchester City went on to win their first ever Women's Super League title, getting their revenge for last year's second place and comfortably finishing above Chelsea with a gap of five points. Although Georgia had to watch from the sidelines at times, she certainly made her mark on the season, and towards the end of July she played some of her best football yet in a

Manchester City shirt. She scored a screamer against Notts County in a 1-5 away win and followed it up a week later with a hat-trick against Sunderland. Georgia scored all three goals in a 3-0 victory and crucially earned her side three points during their fight for the title.

In only a couple of years, Georgia had transformed from an academy prospect to a valued member of the Manchester City team. She had won two trophies and couldn't wait to win more. All she wanted was the chance to get on the football pitch and play to the best of her abilities. It was obvious to anyone who saw her just how much Georgia loved the game. Despite her young age, Georgia played with an excitement blended with fearlessness. It was a deadly combination that was proving to be unstoppable even at the highest level of the game.

8

ENGLAND DEBUT

While Georgia was rising through the
divisions of the women's game the
football world was keeping a close
eye on her, including coaches for the
England national team. Georgia was
often invited to train and play with
the England youth teams – squads

created so that the best young players across the country could train and develop together. This provided a chance for Georgia to continue to train and learn alongside the country's best. It was a group that she thoroughly deserved to be a part of.

Georgia played in tournaments with England's WU17s, WU19s and WU20s. She was even the captain of the WU19s, helping her country and teammates achieve an impressive third place finish in the UEFA European Women's U19 Championship.

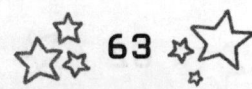

Georgia had played her part for England's youth teams, made strides in the first team at Manchester City, and had done enough to earn herself a place in the England team.

Georgia was announced as a member of the England national team squad for two friendlies in late 2018. Something that would be an incredibly proud moment for anyone, let alone a player who was still only nineteen years old. With three years of experience under her belt, it was easy to forget just how young Georgia was. She would be

one of the youngest in the squad, but Georgia wasn't worried. She had proved she could do it in the Women's Super League, but she was ready to prove that she could perform on an international stage.

The first friendly was an away match, so Georgia had to travel with the squad to Austria where England would be facing off against the Austrians in the nation's capital of Vienna. Phil Neville, the England manager at the time, wanted to use this friendly as an opportunity to test new blood. He also firmly believed that injecting some fresh faces into the national team setup would inspire excitement and confidence in the team. And he did exactly that. Neville gave debuts to Chioma Ubogagu and Georgia, two of the newest members of the squad. The pair were being given a chance straight away to show the world exactly what they could do.

From the start of the match, Georgia was a thorn in the opponent's side, initially firing in a long-range strike that just whistled past the post. She made sure to find pockets of space to create trouble and chaos for Austria. Georgia sent a through ball to Toni Duggan, who took on the shot. The Austrian goalkeeper, Manuela Zinsberger, was only just able to palm away the powerful effort. Georgia and England were knocking firmly on the door, and it was clear that they were going to break through sooner rather than later.

In the 26th minute, the Austrian defence were unable to clear a cross from Karen Carney. Under pressure, the ball kindly fell to the feet of Georgia's fellow debutant,

Ubogagu, who made the most of this gift. The attacker fired the ball past the goalkeeper and into the net. It was 0-1.

But after this goal, the match turned into an edgy contest. Neither side were able to find the second goal in the remainder of the first half or even the start of the second. The clock was ticking, and England were still holding onto their 0-1 lead, but the match was far from over.

In the 72nd minute, Parris made a run down the right wing. Georgia sprinted to join her and arrived in the centre of the box between two defenders. Parris found Georgia with a delicate pass and Georgia saw her chance to score on her England debut. For a moment, it seemed she had missed her opportunity, as Georgia didn't quite connect with the shot. Instead of firing into the back of the net, she had cushioned the ball and it was looping high. But then her lobbed effort dipped and landed in the top right-hand corner. *Goal!* The players celebrated together with a grinning Georgia. She couldn't believe it; not only had she made her national team debut, but she had scored in the match too. And she wasn't finished yet. Georgia provided an assist for Rachel Daly to close out the tie with a third goal in the 81st minute, helping England to a well-deserved 0-3 victory.

If Neville was looking to shake up his squad, he had certainly done that. And now he had a lot of important decisions to make. In 2019, England would be competing in the SheBelieves Cup and the World Cup. And Neville would need to name his squad for those tournaments. There was no doubt that Georgia had given an impressive performance, but it was still only her first appearance. It was an incredible start, but she still had much to learn. Had Georgia done enough to earn a spot in the squad?

SHEBELIEVES
CUP

In the Spring of 2019, England were
invited to compete in the SheBelieves
Cup, a round-robin style tournament
contested by four national teams.
Georgia had done enough to keep
herself in the picture and was included
in the squad for the invitational

tournament. England were going to be playing in matches against Japan, Brazil and USA, the hosts of the competition. They were in with a chance of winning, but the overwhelming favourites were USA. The team were the current World Cup champions and were always a force to be reckoned with. USA would also be playing on home soil in front of thousands of supporters, which was always seen as an advantage. But England were determined to give their all in this competition and to try with all their might to wrestle the cup from its holder.

England's first match
of the tournament was
against Brazil and took place at the
Talen Energy Stadium in Chester,
Pennsylvania with an evening
kick-off. It was the same stadium
where the fans had watched the
opening fixture of the competition
just a handful of hours earlier. The
tournament opener had been a
match between USA and Japan. It
had finished as a 2-2 draw thanks to a
last gasp equaliser from Japan's Yuka
Momiki. This meant that the winner
from this game would immediately

leap to the top of the leaderboard following the first round of fixtures.

Georgia had been named on the bench and so had been told to watch the first match. Although an incredibly talented young player, it was always going to be tough for Georgia to make her way into a team filled with established stars. But she still longed to be included. She knew that the exposure to international football would put her in a good place to thrive in future tournaments. In the meantime, Georgia was determined to learn everything she could. She watched closely as her teammates fought hard for a 2-1 victory. Brazil took an early lead, thanks to a coolly taken penalty from Andressa, but strikes from Ellen White and Beth Mead ensured that England finished the opening day with three points, and an enviable position at the top of the leaderboard.

England's second match in the tournament was expected to be their toughest. They were facing USA in front of 22,125 fans at the Nissan Stadium in Nashville, Tennessee. Georgia and England knew that the majority of the fans in attendance would be supporting USA and hopeful of victory, but they weren't going to let this stop them. England were going to do everything they could to ensure they spoilt the party in the USA.

Supported by a loud crowd, USA took the lead in the 33rd minute, thanks to a goal from Megan Rapinoe which sent the fans into a frenzy. However, England refused to be beaten, and it didn't take long for them to retaliate. The England captain,

Houghton, equalised just three minutes later with a powerful header following a corner. After a chaotic handful of minutes, the two sides were back where the match had started, heading for one point each and determined to get the better of the other side. The pressure was on.

England silenced the home crowd even further in the 52nd minute, as Parris grabbed a second goal for England to put them in the lead. But USA fought back with everything they had. Tobin Heath grabbed an equaliser for USA in the 67th minute.

In an effort to help turn the tide, Neville gave a delighted Georgia her first minutes of the tournament as a substitute. She was determined to do everything she could to take the pressure off her team. And she did exactly that. When the whistle finally blew, both sides left the pitch shaking hands and with one point each.

England were so close to lifting their first ever SheBelieves Cup, but there was still one more match to play. There were still points on offer for all four sides that would play a crucial role in deciding who emerged victorious.

On the final day of the tournament, England faced off against Japan.

 The Lionesses lined up at the Raymond James Stadium in Tampa, Florida ready to fight and play to the very best of their abilities. England knew that if they could win this match, they would be crowned as SheBelieves champions.

England were able to leave their

fear and nerves behind in the opening thirty minutes. The Lionesses scored not once, not twice, but three times, giving themselves a comfortable 0-3 lead thanks to goals from Lucy Staniforth, Carney and Mead. With the team winning comfortably, Neville made changes to ensure other members of the squad got some minutes in their legs. Georgia was one of the players brought onto the pitch and was over the moon to be able to help her country close out the match and claim the victory. England were the

SheBelieves Cup champions for the first time since the competition's creation.

WORLD CUP 2019

As well as progressing with the England national team, Georgia had been playing exceptionally well for her club. She was becoming an integral player for the team and was named on the team sheet more often than not. Manchester City were unable to win the 2018/2019 Women's Super League, but Georgia helped her team win both of the domestic cups. She scored in a 3-0 victory against West Ham in the FA Cup final, as well as scoring in a penalty shootout against Arsenal to claim the League Cup too. Georgia's incredible season had also earned her the PFA's Young Player of the Year Award.

With her impressive performances for Manchester City, and her development within the England national side, Neville knew he had to include her. Georgia was selected as a squad member for the World Cup! She couldn't believe it. She was going to take part in her first ever major international tournament. Georgia was determined to prove to Neville that he had made the right decision. England had shown that they were a side to be reckoned with in the SheBelieves Cup, but could they carry that momentum with them into the World Cup in France?

England had been placed in Group D, competing against Scotland, Argentina and Japan for a place in the knock-out rounds. England kept their energy up as they defeated all three teams to progress out of the group. Georgia made appearances in all of the ties, helping her country perform well in the tournament.

England comfortably made their way past the Round of 16, defeating Cameroon 3-0 thanks to goals from Houghton, White and Alex Greenwood. Georgia didn't take part in this match, but she supported her teammates from the bench and did everything she could to support them throughout the game.

It was at this point that the team really started to believe they could go all the way. England had another 3-0 win in the quarterfinals, easily dispatching Norway thanks to goals from Scott, White and Bronze. Georgia was substituted onto the pitch and was proud to be part of this emphatic win. However, they knew the next match wouldn't be as straightforward. England had been drawn against USA in the semi-finals. The American team were the favourites for the competition and also had a chip on their shoulder after losing the SheBelieves Cup. It was time for one of the biggest matchups of the tournament. The favourites versus the emerging super stars. Which team would come out on top?

It was USA who struck first. Kelly O'Hara fired in a cross that was met by a powerful header from Kristen Press. England's goalkeeper, Bardsley, dived for the ball but was unable to prevent it from crossing the line. It was 1-0 to the USA. But their lead didn't last for too long. England struck back through the help of

their in-form striker, White. Like the opener, Mead curled a cross into the box, while White quickly darted in between two defenders and prodded the ball past the USA's Alyssa Naeher. It was 1-1, and the match was level again.

In the 31st minute, the USA's Lindsey Horan chipped the ball into the penalty area. Alex Morgan, USA's famous forward who was celebrating her 30th birthday, climbed highest and restored her side's lead. The USA were now winning the match 2-1.

England tried as hard as they
could, but they were unable to breach
the USA's defence. They pushed and
pushed, even earning a penalty late
in the game, but Houghton's shot
was saved by Naeher in goal. Georgia
was substituted onto the pitch for
the final few minutes, but it was too
late for her to be able to make an
impact. As the final whistle blew the
England players fell to their knees in
disappointment while the
USA celebrated. Georgia
was gutted, but also
incredibly proud of herself

and her team. She had helped her side get within touching distance of a major trophy. But she wanted more. Georgia wanted to help the Lionesses win their first ever major international trophy.

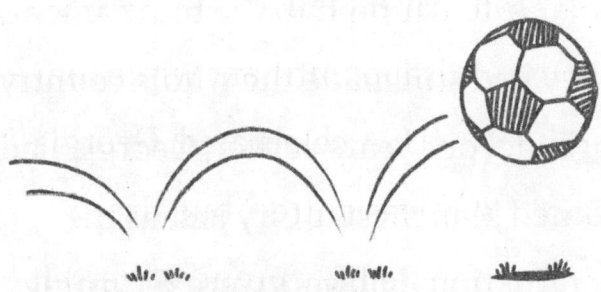

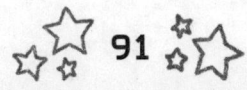

11
GOODBYE ENGLAND

Georgia returned to Manchester City
as a hero. While England had been
unable to triumph in the tournament,
they had still made the whole country
proud. Four years earlier, Georgia had
joined Manchester City just as the
international players were returning

from the 2015 World
Cup. Now she was the
England player returning to camp
in order to carry on with her club's
next season. She was the player who
academy players and young girls
across the country now looked up
to. Just as she had once looked up to
her footballing idols when she was
growing up in Barrow.

Georgia returned to her club ready
to shake off the loss in the World
Cup. She was more than ready to
help her club succeed and to add
more cups to Manchester City's

trophy cabinet. And of course, she wanted more personal recognition, to break more records and add to her collection of winner's medals.

Georgia carried her impressive form from the previous season into the 2019/2020 campaign. She helped Manchester City fight for the Women's Super League crown as well as challenging in the FA Cup, League Cup and Champions League. But then something happened that no one in the world could have predicted. On the 13th of March

2020, the Women's Super League was brought to a halt due to the COVID-19 pandemic. Most of the world was plunged into lockdown, and everything, including football, stopped as the virus took hold. Georgia was determined to keep busy. She trained and followed activities set by her club in order to keep fit at home, wanting to make sure that she would be in top shape when she was finally able to play again. She was also part of a video with fellow Lionesses Bronze, Greenwood and Jordan Nobbs to urge people across the UK to

stay home and stop COVID-19 from spreading.

At the early close of the Women's Super League, Manchester City were sitting in first place in the division. But as they had played one more game than their title challengers, Chelsea, it was decided that the league should be awarded on sporting merit, calculating the final points tally on a points-per-game basis. This was of course a disappointment for Georgia and Manchester City. But it was a decision that was out of their control. They would never

know if they could have gone on to win the league that season, but they completely understood and respected the decision.

Months passed before football was finally able to resume. Manchester City might have been unable to win the league, but they were still able to add to their trophy collection. With Georgia's help, Manchester City triumphed in the re-arranged FA Cup final against Everton. The game finished 1-1 during ninety minutes, but extra time goals from Georgia and her teammate Janine Beckie meant the final score was 1-3. Manchester City were back-to-back FA Cup winners. It was a feat that the club had never achieved before, and something to be proud of.

However, Manchester City's 2020/2021 campaign was one the team would prefer to forget. The side finished as runners up in the league and were unable to win any domestic trophies. Georgia played well for the team, but it was a year of near misses. The side reached semi-finals and quarter-finals but were unable to make it into a single final. Georgia was frustrated. She had been playing and succeeding with Manchester City for seven years. During her time with the club, she had won trophies, scored countless goals, become the club's record goalscorer, but now she felt that she was no longer learning or developing as a player, goalscorer or anything else. Georgia wanted more for herself. She was still only twenty-three, an age when many other players are just starting their career. But at this point, Georgia had played competitively for seven years. It had been an amazing time filled with goals, trophies and memories that she would cherish forever. But in her heart, Georgia knew the time had come for a change. It was time for Georgia to move to another club.

Of course, there were countless teams desperate to sign one of the best attacking midfield talents in women's football. Georgia considered many offers, but it was a giant of German football that

managed to convince her to move.
It was decided. Georgia was moving
to Bayern Munich.

12

EURO 2022

But there was one small matter that
Georgia had to deal with before
she could complete her move.
England were hosting the 2022 UEFA
European Championships. And as
one of her country's best players,
Georgia was included in the squad to
compete at the tournament.

England were under new leadership for this competition. Sarina Wiegman had been appointed as the manager of the national side. She was a well-known and respected coach who had won the tournament previously as the manager of the Netherlands. There was a good feeling about this tournament. England were the hosts, and the team were playing in fine form. Few dared to say it out loud but there was real hope that this was *the* tournament for the Lionesses. This might just be the team who could do it all.

England were playing in Group A. This meant that they would be facing Austria, Norway and Northern Ireland. They were all extremely capable football teams, but many expected England to emerge victorious from this group. This expectation put a huge amount of pressure on the team, but Georgia and the rest of the side were determined not to let it impact their game.

England kicked off the exciting tournament with their opening day match against Austria. The match was being played at Old Trafford, the home of Manchester United, in front of a staggering crowd of 68,781 fans. It was an enormous audience for a women's football match. For a long time women's football hadn't been treated equally with the men's game, and there are still many inequalities between the two, but there was a different feeling about this tournament. For the first time ever, millions of new fans were being pulled into the magic, talent and beauty of women's football. It appeared that the public were waking up to the enormous skill that the players possessed.

Watched by thousands in the stadium, with many more watching on TV, the Lionesses walked out of the tunnel with their heads held high. The fans roared as the players strode onto the pitch. Everyone could see their steely determination and focus. Georgia was one of the players starting the match and she was ready. This was her, her team's and her country's moment and nothing was going to get in their way. And nothing did. To the delight of the fans, Mead scored for England in the 16th minute and the team went on to win 1-0. This meant they had won the first three points of the tournament, shooting straight up to first place in the group.

England's second group game was against Norway. The side were seen by some as a dark horse for the tournament, and one to be watched. It was expected to be a tough match and a potential stumbling block for the Lionesses. But they had already dealt with their first hurdle, and they had no plans to fall at the second.

Once again, Georgia was named in the starting lineup, and it didn't take long for her to make an impact. In the 10th minute, England were awarded a penalty. White was brought down in the penalty area and the referee pointed to the spot. It was now up to Georgia as England's penalty taker. She had imagined this moment over and over again, but now it was actually happening. Georgia put everything else out of her head and

 focussed. She ran up to the ball and fired it to the left of the goal. The goalkeeper

guessed the right way and dived for the ball. For a second Georgia's heart dropped, but the effort was too powerful and well placed. The back of the net rippled, and England were in the lead. A grinning Georgia celebrated with her teammates. She had just scored her first goal in a major tournament and put her team 1-0 up. However, this was just the start. No one could have predicted what happened next. England simply couldn't stop scoring and went on to defeat Norway 8-0. Not only had they

beaten their opponents, but they had also put down a real marker for the other teams in the tournament.

England signed off their group stage matches in fantastic style with a 0-5 win against Northern Ireland. They had finished in first position in the group which meant they would continue through the tournament into the knock-out rounds.

England's opponents for the quarter-final were Spain. They were known to be a talented team that had been playing well despite going through a tough time. One of Spain's leading talents, Alexia Putellas, had to miss the tournament due to an ACL injury. But the Spanish side were still putting in impressive performances and they did not stop for the England tie. Spain struck first as Esther González fired in the first goal in the 54th minute. The thousands of fans in attendance, who were almost all supporting England, fell silent. Surely their team couldn't lose? Georgia and her team rallied together. They didn't want their tournament to end and needed to find an equaliser. The Lionesses threw everything they had

at Spain. They sent forward attack after attack, but they couldn't find the goal. Time was running out, and it looked like England were going to be defeated. Just when it looked like it was all over, England created a chance.

In the last few minutes of the match, Georgia flicked the ball into the box. Daly brought it under her control and crossed the ball. Alessia Russo rose highest and headed it to the ground before Toone fired the ball into the net. It was 1-1. Inspired by their late equaliser, the England team had hope. For so long it appeared that they were crashing out, but now they had their second chance.

The game went into extra time, and in the 96th minute the ball was given to Georgia in Spain's half. She looked around, but she was surrounded by Spanish defenders and far away from the goal. Yet Georgia was determined to try; she looked up and fired a shot at goal. As her powerful strike zoomed towards the net, the Spanish goalkeeper, Sandra Paños, tried unsuccessfully

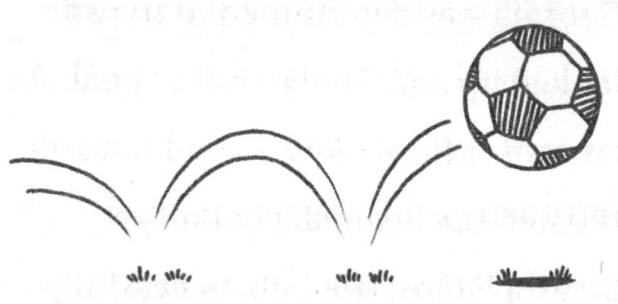

to stop it. Georgia had scored! The stadium erupted with cheers as Georgia and her teammates couldn't stop celebrating. The Lionesses were able to close out the game and, thanks to Georgia's wonderstrike, England were through to the semi-finals.

13
THE PATH TO WEMBLEY

Georgia had saved England's tournament with her incredible extra time strike. As a result of her brilliance England had progressed to the semi-finals of the tournament. Fortunately, this wasn't as tough as the quarter final. The Lionesses

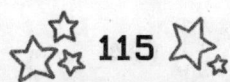

defeated Sweden with a 4-0 victory. As always, Georgia played her part in her team's dominant performance, never letting her form slip and pushing her country ever closer to its first ever European Championship crown.

Before that, there was one more obstacle standing in England's way. The Lionesses were playing against Germany in the final of the UEFA European Championships 2022. It was a match that would be watched by millions across the globe. It was also a match where Georgia would face off against players from her new team.

Georgia would be playing against the likes of Lina Magull, Giulia Gwinn and Klara Bühl, all talented players who were soon to be her teammates. But this was no time to be friendly; for the upcoming match these players were rivals determined to claim victory for their own country and win the trophy.

The England team walked out of the stadium to deafening cheers and applause. The Lionesses were playing a fixture in front of an incredible 87,192 fans. This was the highest ever

attendance in the final tournament of a UEFA men's or women's national team competition. Millions more were watching the match on TV at home, in pubs or gathered together with hundreds of others in a football  park. Every single one of them were crossing their fingers and sitting on the edges of their seats, ready to witness one of the biggest games in the history of women's football.

The referee blew their whistle and the match kicked off. As England and Germany battled it out against one another, trying to figure out the opposing team without making a mistake, it was clear that both teams were desperate to win. This pressure caused both sides to be a little cautious, so it was no surprise that neither side was able to make a breakthrough in the first half. But in the second half, everything changed. A moment of brilliance meant one of the teams was finally able to find the opening goal.

Walsh played a precise long ball over the top of the German defence. Toone, making a darting run, latched onto the ball and ran through on goal. Chased by a defender, and with the goalkeeper closing the space, Toone needed to act fast. She chipped the ball over the onrushing goalkeeper and scored. Georgia rushed over to her teammate to celebrate, as the thousands of fans in attendance leapt out of their seats and cheered as loudly as they could. England had the lead in the World Cup final.

There were just over ten minutes left on the clock, and Germany refused to be beaten. Georgia's soon to be teammate, Magull, scored an equaliser. Her nifty left-footed strike soared over Mary Earps's gloves and into the back of the net. England's earlier excitement was dampened, but this wasn't the end of the road. Once more, Georgia and her teammates rallied together. They could still do this. The match might be level but the game was still in their hands. They just needed to come together for one last push.

As the match continued neither side was able to find a winner and the match went into extra time.

Could anyone step up and save the day?

In the 110th minute England had a corner. Hemp swung the ball in with a powerful cross, and the English attackers rose – as did the German defenders. Bronze was able to get to the ball and she flicked it forwards. The ball bounced onto the ground and no one had cleared it. There was a chance. Chloe Kelly stuck out her foot and poked the ball past the goalkeeper. England were in the lead! If the cheers for the first goal had been loud then these

cheers were deafening. Standing on the edge of the box, ready to deal with any loose balls, Georgia had enjoyed the best view in the stadium, watching from metres away as her teammate scored.

Georgia and her teammates were able to see out the remaining time and to everyone's relief the referee blew her whistle. The players and coaches hugged, cried and cheered on the pitch. They were champions. Georgia and her fellow Lionesses had made history.

14
GEORGIA'S FUTURE

Following her triumph, Georgia is now one of the best attacking midfield players for Bayern Munich. She has become close friends with the players who not so long ago were her enemies in the UEFA final. Although Georgia remembers that match more fondly

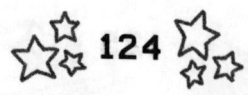

than some of her German teammates.

When joining a new club, football players are often made to sing an initiation song in front of the group. Georgia was no exception and cheekily opted to sing *Sweet Caroline* – the song most associated with English football – in front of a mostly German audience. Her teammates saw the funny side but made sure to chase her after she had finished singing.

Georgia has been taking German lessons ever since her arrival in the country but is yet to master the language despite weekly lessons.

Luckily her coaches and teammates are always happy to practice their English on her. The coach, Alexander Straus, holds his team meetings in English, the training ground instructions are in English and even the WhatsApp group is in English.

There is one thing that Georgia misses about home though, apart from her family and friends. Georgia reckons that German baked beans just don't taste the same as English ones.

Georgia's career would be the envy of any footballer. She's achieved domestic wins, league titles and of course the famous Euros win. But sometimes the losses in football can mean just as much as the victories.

England were runners-up in the 2023 World Cup, but Georgia and her teammates still made their country proud. She had scored an important penalty in their match against Haiti, showing great courage to retake it after a false start and firing the ball into the back of the net.

Although Spain took the trophy home, Georgia and her teammates still played incredibly well.Georgia has certainly come a long way from her days playing football on the Strawberry Grounds. She's made her move from Barrow to Bavaria and has achieved success after success along the way. The young footballer has broken records, played her heart out and done it all with a beaming smile. Georgia still has a lot of football to play, and she will give every upcoming challenge and test her all, while loving every single moment.

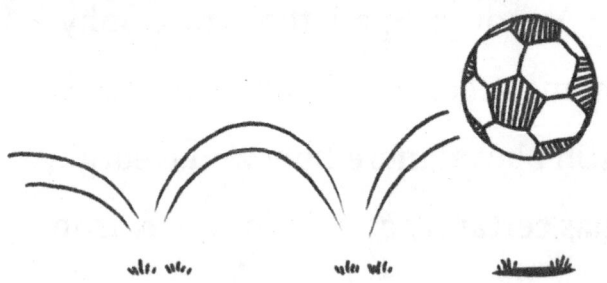